BROKEN COUNTRY

Published in the UK in 2021 by Marinaleda Publishing

Copyright © 2021 Claudia Esposito

The right of Claudia Esposito to be identified as the Author of the Work has been asserted by her in accordance with the Copyright, Designs and Patents Act 1988.

All rights reserved, including the right to reproduce this book, or portions thereof in any form. No part of this text may be reproduced, transmitted, downloaded, decompiled, reverse engineered, or stored, in any form or introduced into any information storage and retrieval system, in any form or by any means, whether electronic or mechanical without the express written permission of the author.

Paperback ISBN: 978-1-8384090-0-5
eBook ISBN: 978-1-8384090-1-2

BROKEN COUNTRY
MEMORIES AND THOUGHTS OF AN ITALIAN ANTI-RACIST

CLAUDIA ESPOSITO

MARINALEDA PUBLISHING

To Aitor, with all my love.
With you by my side everything is possible.

CONTENTS

An Italian Silence 9
There And Back 17
Another Childhood 22
Mini Me 26
In The Mess, Anti-Racism 28
Farouk Kassam Kidnapping In An Italy Which No Longer Exists. 32
The Bubble 36
This Is The Night 40
Here And There 48
Protest And... Protest? 54
Sweet, White Sleeping Beauty 57
Bull Trump And The Day After Tomorrow 61
Another Rebel Day 64
Remembering Neruda 67
Statement Of Defense 70
Interlude. Legality And Rational Thinking: Rapid Approach 74
Tribute To Antipathy (Or About The Tragic Mistake Of Being Good) 76
Another Soldier 82
Cry, Baby Cry 86

AN ITALIAN SILENCE

Like many others I came to the UK looking for a way to put my qualifications and capacities to use. Life was hard in the beginning; I felt I was able to handle it, as I come from a family of immigrants, after all.

My parents moved from a small village near Napoli to the North of Italy.

Despite a deep connection with my Southern roots, I spent most of my life in Padova, a town in Veneto, North East Italy: our little slice of Texas here in the old continent.

During my years there I witnessed more episodes of racism than I can remember.

Italy was "the most beautiful country in the World", the land of the greatest hospitality, the warmest welcome. A land of solidarity, or what Hannah Harendt called our "natural sense of humanity": the spontaneous understanding of other people's needs, feelings and suffering.

Our values, our soul and our future were destroyed by racism. My country and all it represented is no more and we have to fight every day just to remember what we were.

I often wondered what exactly pushed me to move from a country I love so much and for which I, along with many others, faced important battles for our liberties since I was a teenager. We fought against the repression of press freedom during the Berlusconi era, when the most prominent Italian journalist, Michele Santoro, was kicked off national television for questioning the relationship between Berlusconi and the mafia; we fought against the Iraqi war; against the human rights violations in Guantanamo; against racism and inequality. We were committed and happy to fight for Italy.

But time passed and so did our rage and contempt. Year after year, defeat after defeat (corruption trial after mafia trial). It's difficult to tell yourself the truth; we were young and outraged, until we weren't anymore.

The tragic irony of this little country will be forever depicted by Pasolini in his statement "I know, but I don't have any evidence". We know the truth. Whether it' s a complicated web of lies and conspiracies or not, connecting the dots has never been as easy as it is in Italy. Sometimes we don't know all the names, other times we don't get the precise chronology. But we know. That's why it's so difficult for us to get the importance of journalism, which remains such a fundamental part of our democracy. That's because in Italy we just need journalists with the integrity to write and let us know the truth that nobody even bothered to hide almost as much as we need investigative journalists uncovering secret truths on corruption and mafia. In our history the courage to tell us the truth has been way more important than investigative journalism, which is usually destined to deal with facts and crimes better explored by prosecutors and their subsequent trials. So, most of the time it's not about "asking the right questions", but being independent enough to let people know the answers. It's a moral issue. I have faith we will prevail against mafia and corruption, but to do so we need to address this main problem. The moral duty of a journalist is to tell the truth and keep citizens informed and ready to take their decision in the polls, whatever that decision may be.

Therefore journalism is just one sector of our society in which the loss of any moral decency has been most obvious. The very same immoral attitude can be seen everywhere. I don't think Berlusconi and his deranged tendency to bribe journalist, politicians, judges and slander everybody else are the sole causes of this wrong turn. We all remember Leonardo Sciascia in "gli zii di Sicilia" and the memorable description of people throwing their Fascist Party membership cards off the roof when they saw the North American tanks approaching, just to make sure they would be able to take it back if the Fascists returned. But I do think Berlusconi took it to another level. No one in the '90s was driven by the will to survive a war and the ending of a dictatorship that didn't bring any good and , according to our profound common sense, was not worth dying for. It was a whole different thirst for wealth at any cost; for money no matter what. Common sense where it's needed became indifference to any choice and its moral significance. Year after year, we spent decades listening to entire sections of politics and society destroying our faith in the Constitution, the judiciary, the institutions. A Sicilian mafia-affiliated man labelled "hero" by a Prime Minister: what else do you need to unleash your greed and live free from the rules that should make us a community? It was a slow, pathetic, tacky descent into the dark place where we now are. A few years ago after the last earthquake in central Italy, two constructors were caught by police laughing while the dust was still settling . People were still alive under the rubble and the constructors were laughing loudly on the phone, talking of the good business they were about to do thanks to that tragedy. It broke our hearts, but how many of us were honestly surprised by that? The profound disrespect for life and the absence of any decency is revealed in that laughter, if you want to ask yourself how Italians became what they are today. They are immoral. Indifferent, cruel. And, of course, racists.

Racism was definitely what contributed the most to my deep disaffection for my Italian daily life and made me leave. Italy, the *Bel Paese*, the country of the fascinating Sicily, the wonderful Sardegna or Dolomiti mountains, country of ancient and beloved culinary traditions, which is today one of the most racist countries in Europe. I could see this particularly clearly since I came to live abroad. When something about Italy becomes part of the collective foreign imagery to the point of being mentioned almost as much as "mafia," we have acquired another cliché which the country of pizza really needed.

But when I was living in Italy what I had to experience every day was my normality. It was not only the aggressions, the violence or the insults. It was the daily subtle tension in every place you happened to be. The forced silence around you. The constant attempt to avoid, prevent, and pretend. The number of times in one day you have to whisper yourself "Keep going. Don't stop, don't argue or you are going to be here for the next half an hour and you can't. No children, no people in need. Look at them, they're doing great. Just carry on, just this time..". It didn't really work very often for me. After arguing, defending, accusing, shouting and sometimes even crying, I used to check how much time it took me to step in, stop the aggression and go back to what I was doing. Every time was faster than the previous one, I was proud to note. Timing is crucial in a situation where every black person passing by is potentially a walking episode of racism.

Other than the violence, the aggressions and harrassment, racists in Italy are perfectly entitled to praise discrimination and each other's prejudices openly, because we are all supposed to agree. It's baffling.

"I am not racist but..." is an example of the most exhausting dumb idiocy you have to listen to. Italians are so accustomed to these words that it's not even a disclaimer anymore. It's lifestyle. It's no longer the excuse we use to complain about things immigrants are believed to do, no. It's an expression of gentle confidence thinly disguised behind the smiling face of a middle-class man who's speaking the most horrific lies about Black people, insulting your intelligence and human decency, with the calm that allows him to be considered a moderate by everyone who listens. Except you. You, drinking your beer avidly, suddenly wanting to kill yourself to avoid the abominable consequences of another bad decision: that of hanging out with other Italians. I cast my mind back to a day in January 1944. People just like these ones watched their Jewish friends and neighbours walking in a procession of thousands from the city prison through the streets of Milano towards the infamous Platform 21 of the rail station, to be deported to Auschwitz. No one looked out from the window, no one said a word. No one did anything. They were "not racist, but.." .. but you know, they're Jewish, we're not; they're Jewish, who knows. It was the peace of Nazis, with no swastika behind their windows, but an inhuman talent for indifference towards the destiny of others. Today's racism is the echo and legacy of the same bland indifference. Racism is so easy, so at the ready for everybody to blame someone else for everything. It's the magic of it. No need to understand, no need to make an effort to see what's going on around you. No need to think. I've heard people blaming immigrants for their son's inability to to find a job while smiling and looking at him, someone I can't help but define as the dumbest, laziest, most ignorant, useless, drug-addicted loser I have ever seen in my life. Glorious. If you smile thinking of something else for long enough maybe you can find the meaning of life. It' s my personal yoga, but with tequila. No need to water it down. Also, racism is a big unifier. It unifies different kinds of people who have one thing in common: the need to hide something and divert the attention to someone weaker, alone, incapable of any large- scale, coordinated defense. Let's see.

A huge number of restaurants and bar-owners in Veneto evade taxes with the help of the corrupt authority which is supposed to collect them. Patronage and corruption rule universities and the many other institutions for which it's impossible to work unless you have a connection with someone who will guarantee you're not going to question the system precisely because you're part of it. And last but not least, those involved in crimes related to criminal organizations' interest in public sectors. People in Veneto have a lot to lose from a world free of racism. The dirt needs to be hidden while lying in plain sight.

So, the great solution. One for all of them, or seriously did no-one never notice the exhausting silence of conservative catholics towards racism ?

Forget everything. Blame the immigrants. Blame the blacks. Blame the muslims. Blame them.

And that's why all the residents of a little town felt able to refuse to host fifteen women and children, refugees from war. Or a group of fascists gathered before an apartment assigned by the local city council to a poor Romani family. The children cried, frightened by the shouts and insults. The father enters the house with his children, he's crying too. He cries and ask why so much hate for a family, for these children? He doesn't know. Me neither.

Yet all the while your sons get coked up with your money and travel to Thailand, or Romania, or Africa, where in some regions signs written in Italian say "Don't touch the children." Those people need racism to detract from the human misery they spread around simply by crossing the threshold. It was difficult to live in Veneto because of the racism I witnessed and tried to counter everyday, and also because the perpetrators give you so many reasons to feel so disgusted and repelled by them. Another tiresome insanity is "I think you're exaggerating things…". Our community has a great influence on us, good or bad. When I realized who I was surrounded with I started being hypercritical, questioning every idea they tried to force into my mind. When I was very young I used to say "I disagree" before knowing why. I used to figure out why just afterward. I never regretted it.

So, as a result of being an anti-racist, you become weird to them: the stubborn one: the one who's impossible to persuade. In their words, they're not trying to make you racist. They're just trying to make you reasonable. Then you choose: give a more accommodating image of yourself or, if you can endure it, forget all the useful lessons about the value of compromising and go your own way. So you hang out with people, you pass by, you go to a party but there is no place you don't find someone with the urge to let you know how much they hate you and what you think. You just go away. And then, you go away again. And again. I learned to proceed through life independently and that was crucial in order to avoid being engulfed by the nonsense they threw at me constantly. And the cowardice. Oh my. The endless cowardice of a racist. I lived for thirty years in Veneto. I remember few aggressive attitudes towards Black men. Instead, the attacks, the violence and injustice I saw in public spaces were almost every time directed at Black women. Often young women with little children witnessing the episode, watching their mother be called names, almost always by white men, sometimes by old women. I stopped thinking long ago of elderly people as our history and guardians of our ancient values. Sometimes they are just old people, as evil today as their younger versions were decades ago. I think of the men I've met in England. British men, Spanish or East Timor guys, and men from many other countries. After thirty years in Veneto, the delivery guy and the greengrocer look like British Lords just appointed by the Queen.

I do understand how difficult it is not to think "racism" when you think of Italy. No one can appreciate the magic landscapes of Toscana or the treasures in our museums when they know what happens in the streets and that you have to be white and racist yourself in order to forget who Italians have become and content to enjoy our hospitality despite that. Obviously racism is nasty always and everywhere. But everything is so much more painful when it happens in your own country. That life, day by day, made me feel alone, unable to change the situation and I felt the need to be myself outside a book, a room, or a house. Out in the open, away from my land and the life I was living there. Maybe find a better way than lone anger to fight for a change. Living in England is like coming out of a bad nightmare. I wake up, everyday, surrounded by more people than haters. No place is safe from that poison. Nevertheless, I look around and I know everybody is safe; men and women just living their lives, moving around you, errands, school, work, dreams. I look at the face of a man without asking myself if he's someone likely to attack a woman in front of her children, in public, in front of the many turning their face on the other side, like a window slammed shut in that awful, Nazi silence.

THERE AND BACK

Like many southerners we also went to visit our family in the South, every summer. The first morning we used to wake up, still tired from the long trip and my mother would dress me and my sister and bring us to "the other grandmother", the mother of my father.

It was a huge place full of possibilities for fun for two little girls. The kitchen had an interior door to the little groceries store they had owned for decades, so my grandmother used to spend the day in the kitchen and when people came into the store they shouted "Teresa, come here!"

Grandma's house had seen lives, seasons, ages; from the '60s when villagers brought their own chairs into the living room to watch the show on the only channel, on the first and only television in town; to the '70s and the motley army of girlfriends with which her sons slept in sleeping bags scattered here and there on the three floors of the house.

Then man went to the moon and that evening Grandma leant out of the door and took a look at the moon, hoping to see something.

A couple of her sons lived in a farmhouse in the countryside, right out of town; one day one of them climbed onto the roof of the Salesian college to leave some marjiuana to dry . Our youngest uncle of the six, Franco, was 12 at the time and had fun helping his older brother, even if he didn't actually know what was all that about - yet.

Grandma used to sit right out of the door, as is the custom in our small towns, and one day suddenly a young boy passed by running in front of her. She sighed, a little resigned and a little amused. After few seconds one of her sons stormed down the street and flew behind the first one; just long enough to scuffle and then he was home, all dishevelled and sweaty. But the following day he was all dressed up, in his best suit, to pick up his girlfriend from school and bring her home.

Then the '80s arrived and everything that could have gone wrong surely did, and at great speed.

I didn't know what happened or why Franco never slept in town; it seemed weird and cruel, as if everybody resented him.

For all of us, daughters of his brothers, Franco was the puppy/uncle we wanted to cuddle, because nobody else did. None of us recalled what he did wrong, but his distance from the other adults made him closer to us, playful and fun. We were annoyed by people being condescending with him, but it was a joy to have him all to ourselves.

Once he took the old blue Renault Diane with me, my sister and our cousin Chiara on the back seats. After thousands of recommendations and reassurances to my father that it would be a supposedly small trip and pastoral panorama, he turned the corner and started driving as though he was navigating an invisible chicane. We cried with wide-open mouths, our flushed red cheeks facing the back window.

Dangerous, even by 1980s standards. A lot of fun, though.

Those carefree moments meant so much to me. They distracted me from my troubled thoughts. There was something in my heart of hearts which I didn't properly understand and fazed me, in these years. A subtle feeling, crawling and inexplicable, for a child. Like a stomach activates to digest nutrients, through that heart flowed raking emotions, but it couldn't process or explain them. It was a powerful catalyst for my thoughts but I was too young to process answers. And so the sky during the sunset, stray dogs howling all night long or the deafening cicadas in the summer afternoons; all these little things made me almost cry, or think about death. I had this disturbing sense of being a dot in the flow of time leading me to overthink the past, present and future. I often remained in the garden alone, dozing in the rocking chair, wondering what this feeling of distress and sadness was. I indulged in the feeling of looking for an answer though I didn't know words such as "depression" or "melancholy". I lost track of time. Then I saw my little sister in pursuit of a big stray cat and I woke up to help her. I threw little rocks towards him, blocking his way on my side and when he was running back my sister, with a bit of luck, could catch and hold him in her sweet, unsolicited hug.

So it was relaxing for me having always something to do, being busy with people and toys and our little adventures. I imagine it's where it all started: my sleep problems, my hatred of silence, my need to be constantly busy with doing something.

The first days were the most difficult. At my "other Grandma's" house, that first morning of every summer, I delivered kisses to whoever was around and then I walked away into the living room. I sat on the oldest couch I've ever seen, and is still unbeaten by any other. I sniffed the air swinging my legs. A strange smell of wet dust, mould hidden behind the furniture, and the dirty leather of worn-out purses and suitcases piled up in a corner. An antique brush left on a 80's printer next to a piece of pencil and the key of a locker. The antique crystal-drops chandelier swung when the door opened and I looked out to see if someone interesting had just arrived.

I wanted to come back to my Grandma-Grandma, the mother of my mother. It was not only her cooking or how funny it was to stay with her and listen to her stories or the walks along the river-bank and all the many other things we did with her. It occurred to me, sometimes, that we were living in the "after": after the war, after the funny tales about this person or another, after the incredible things you could do when my parents were young. It seemed we were living a time when everything had already happened. But with my Grandma-Grandma, we had fun and people had fun with us. It was our time, mine and my sister's. A time we would have remembered. A time no one was talking about, but that one day we would have to tell to the future children of our family. A time we too were part of.

Everyday my sister and I decided with whom to spend the day. We were with my grandparents when an old lady headed to the cemetery passed by and we went with her; her son and his girlfriend brought us back home where we found our favourite aunt, the girlfriend of my mother's brother. So I went with her to visit her parents, until my uncle came to pick her up and we spent the night with them. My parents sometimes lost track of our moving. They needed a couple of phone calls to figure out where we were and bring us back home.

I counted the days left we had to come back home, whether they were many or few. We knew that we still had many days to spend with Grandma if there was no water and we could have a bath just using the water collected from the tap in the garden. Grandma warmed it up in a big pot and poured it over our heads. I knew there were only a few days left when we had water almost every day.

With September approaching we had water almost every day and I know we were about to go back home to the North.

In those last days the air was fresher and I had to take out my books and start my holiday homework. The smell of the pencil, the rubber, all these things recalled me to where and what I was about to come back to. My heart was heavy while I swung my little legs on the wicker chair. At my grandmother's house I didn't know where to leave my pencil case, there was no place for my backpack or the thought of all the contempt

I was subject to at school. In the midst of a shallow tiredness I took comfort in the thought that I would always come back.

I went to school, I played with very few friends, waiting to come back home, to where I never actually lived, the only house I've ever had.

ANOTHER CHILDHOOD

I am the daughter of two old communists and that's affected my path very much. My parents were also southerners, from the province of Caserta, so while they were trying to give me and my sister a good education as all parents would do, their example and beliefs felt so strong and present in our lives that I rapidly turned into something they didn't really expect or actually want. They were very skeptical and diffident about every issue or idea which wasn't related to politics or didn't have an educational purpose. Somehow, I never felt that as problematic, for me. Surrounded by people and habits so different from us, southerners in the deep North of Italy, everything coming from my parents seemed an affirmation of diversity, our diversity, and I was ok with it.

    I was allowed to go to bed later to watch the Michele Santoro show but my mother didn't say or explain anything to me when I had my first period. She seemed a bit embarassed, telling me in her kindest possible way: "Well, ok. Now you have to wash yourself very often". She briefly shown me how to use the pads and she went back to the kitchen. There was some sort of bigotry in this behavior, but it can be difficult to identify bigotry when it doesn't come from a conservative environment. My mother, coming from a small village in the South of Italy, grew up finding it difficult to talk about anything related to sex. This southern blanket of deep silence was not wiped off by communism. Quite the opposite. It was probably comforting for her to know that there was, somewhere out there far from her small village, someone fighting for a justice she never experienced, as a woman or a citizen. I imagine she found a new sense of freedom, but I know for sure she also found a new framework of rules in which she could feel safe, her life framed in a pre-conceived pattern to be followed. Personal issues were not labelled as "essential " by the communist orthodoxy, so she never really felt the need to explain any such thing to me, or to make me ask questions or express feelings. Communism was hope and, what's more, not a challenge for her catholic backward education. Somehow, she passed from one bigotry to another.

My father could spend the entire dinner explaining to me who the Gava in Napoli were, but never asked me what I did with my friends the night before, or discussed the meaning of a movie. I was encouraged to read his old books about the CIA activity in Vietnam, but I was not allowed to ask to buy heels because, as my mother solemnly stated, "fascists wear heels". My heels were always cheap shoes bought with a friend of mine in the worst shop in town, hidden in a corner of the closet. When she thought I forgot that I had them, my mother threw them away without telling me. The worst part is that I was never too upset about it, because deep inside me lay the idea that those heels were the sign of my wrongful rebellion against our sacred fight against injustice. I usually wore them just while hanging out with my best friend. Otherwise, specially at school, I wore more leftist outfits (sic). Even in the mess of the teenage years defection never crossed my mind. They were our ideas. Politics in my family had nothing to do with your personal beliefs. Communists were fighters, proud in victory and (more frequently) defeat, while evil wealthy individuals were oppressing humanity, denying justice. Fighters don't defect. They listen, they learn, they follow.

I listened and learned and followed until I was old enough to form what I saw as a personalisation of what I'd heard about since I was a child. They were exciting new years of afternoons spent in the bookshops. The stories I wanted to read were by authors my parents didn't know anything about.

My parents knew most of their cultural background was strictly related to Marxism and part of classic literature was missing. I still remember their simple, beautiful wisdom. I recall my father and I in a big bookshop, me jumping happy between the shelves while he waited patiently and silently behind me, letting me discover my own path towards awareness, politics, love.

I still love reading fiction and my parents are very proud of me because of this, but my father never read a single book I suggested to him from my precious collection. When I gave him American Pastoral by Robert Roth, one of my favourite masterpieces, he leafed through the book gently smiling, like you do when you're looking at something that can certainly be entertaining, but not seriously relevant. I looked at the face of the only man I ever loved; the only individual whose opinion was meaningful to me. I realized then, in a single second, that we were different. We were connected, but not like a soul in two different bodies. It was freedom, with a hint of loneliness, and this feeling of an infinite amount of books, choices, decisions I could have made, but outside of my actual framework, which wasn't communism or that romantic (although elitist) love some of my relatives had for southern Italy and its ancient traditions. My father was my framework, my context. And out there, out of my father's safe world, I needed to look for my communism, my South, my set of rules. My bigotry.

It's not easy to realize that. How can you properly discern the limits of those two individuals, born in one of the most dangerous and lawless places of our South, who arrived in the North alone and unwanted, who lived every day of their lives defying stereotypes, learning the new without forgetting the old, with no simplistic hate for the many immigrants fighting for their families the same daily war they were fighting?

For quite a while I felt so guilty, facing the growing and crystal-clear gap between them and me. But beyond filial love and a sense of loss, I needed to make my framework more personal, adjusted to suit my feelings, my experiences and my opinions.

Sometimes he made me laugh. Who cares if his hair is green, he's so amazing, so kind, smart! Not everything must have a political meaning! My father showed off his stubborness by just conceding his irrationality with a quick smile: - Green. Please.

But at the same time he couldn't conceive of a World in which I was considered less than someone else for being a woman. Even more than my mother, probably, ignoring what a woman can actually experience, he pushed me to be the best I could and not be afraid to show it, to claim what is mine without excuses and shyness. He made me fearless.

What a strange universe must live in his head. Southerner, silent, rational, passionate, Marxist, sweet family man and resilient anti- fascist. Today, I just love him this way. And no: I didn't grow up to perfection. I am also looking for my orthodoxy, haven't found it yet. Maybe I never will . The framework of my safety. Sometimes I just think it's there, between a condescending smile and a father waiting behind me in a library: trying to pass me his best and let me discover what he missed.

MINI ME

My upbringing was not demanding. I used to feel happily involved in our fight for justice, making my contribution with my several protests against private property such as rugs, glass-made collectibles, mechanical and electronic devices; not to mention my commitment against the middle-class obsession for hygiene. After bringing destruction and despair to the home of the uncle or a family friend, though, I was in line with my sister to be dressed, kissed by each and everyone in the room, say goodbye and leave. I was great at being kissed; promptly offering my cheek and waving to everyone, standing still for a head pat, smiling until the very last pinch on the nose. We were part of something bigger and I was there doing my part for justice. Discipline, man.

In Italy some embittered, deluded ex-communists used to say "you're born leftist, you die conservative". I looked at those disillusioned and pessimist people with a masterful, faraway look since I was very young . A little snotty me. I couldn't tell them, I was just a kid, but I snubbed them awfully even though they never noticed. I ignored them, with contempt. Maybe, underneath my lively, light-hearted appearance I wasn't the nicest kid, but I had unwavering beliefs. I had a road and so I felt safe everywhere I was, never afraid because our ideals would spread over every aspect of my life, comforting me in every situation. I was never a frightened child and I gave vent to my curiosity without much thought. It was beautiful.

Someone may say this sense of safety had a price, because having unshakable beliefs means also having a designated path: opinions, interests, everything was marked by what we believed in. But isn't it like that for everybody, every time, everywhere?

The truth is that no matter what our ideas are, they affect us deeply. Even the apparent conformist emptiness of the many young girls using their bodies as a virtual product to sell on the social networks is actually a clear decision to screw politics and live in an eternal present, leaving the crucial choices to other (mostly male) individuals. This is an attitude stemming from a profoundly conservative and bigoted perspective on women and their social status, on politics and justice, things that exist only for those who have them already.

The fact that my political and personal path would be externally more regimented in no way detracts from the fanaticism of modern indifference.

It was a world of rules, but they were fair rules, for they were devoted to a just cause and following them gave sense to my life. We had to be seriously committed to do our best at any time, careful about what was right to do or to say and what wasn't, but we didn't mind.

The rules some young people want to get rid of nowadays are rules whose meaning is unappreciated or no longer exists. Our rules had meaning and purpose. I was very proud: blindly proud, dogmatically happy.

Of course, I grew up. Different moments came to me. Doubts, critiques, changes, diversions. Nevertheless still today, in these uncertain pandemic days, I hold on to few clear rules: I stick to the rules I understand the reasons for; I constantly remind myself that being alone is not being wrong. I work on being opinionated, I take a stand. I don't step back from a just fight. I am what I think. I don't allow myself the option of a convenient surrender. Fight, fight from your eternal state of opposition, for every good cause and forever. It's the most beautiful quality of an old geezer communist.

IN THE MESS, ANTI-RACISM

So I grew up happy. Believing in something is not complicated. It probably simplifies life: it certainly simplified my childhood.

I wonder how my parents lived (fully, instead of me) in the difficult Italian '80s; the end of the '70s and domestic Marxist terrorism and the "strategy of tension", the political disengagement, a Cold War which seemed eternal but instead was about to end. I didn't know any of that.

I woke up in the morning, crawled under the blanket while my mother opened the window wide to refresh the air. With the duvet pulled up to my nose I looked at the wall and the child was there, like every morning. He stared at me with his tired but smiling glance, his head wrapped in a weird black and white scarf. His small raised hand made the sign of victory.

When I learnt to read and I recalled the child, I ran into my room to find out what was written on that poster, under the picture of the child: "We could all...die but if one preg.. preg-nant woman remains, she will give birth to a child that will free Pp... Palestine.". The signature said "anonymous on a wall of Beirut".

I thought I had so much luck with everything I got. It didn't matter how tiny your world was , it was anyway part of something bigger and that was reassuring and exciting at the same time. Plus we had a lot of beautiful songs to sing in the car. Do the other kids have songs as great as ours ? I didn't think so. We sang Inti Illimani marching up and down the house in single file behind my mother to welcome my father coming home from work. Could the other kids do so? I didn't believe so.

Political engagement was permanent and everywhere but, of course, I lived in different moments, as happens in everybody's life. Naive, upset, shy, thoughtful. We were however part of that working class which you only heard about in other areas of the city. It was difficult to feel comfortable in my well-known high-school. I attended my classes, revolving around the world that lived in it. My social and political microcosm wasn't there and I didn't complain. The youth around me was preparing to become a more sarcastic, cynical and antirevolutionary elite than their parents. I didn't come from one of those families. Down in my neighbourhood, politics could upset you for much longer than a demonstration. Our economic problems kept talking to me after the stump speech depicting the demarcation line between me and my schoolmates. Thus some kind of solitude always ruled my mind.

Young students protesting in the streets didn't come back home with me, through the derelict neighbourhoods where our first immigrants lived scraping for food. They didn't see the first frightening violent incidents which I still remember today. Maybe they were missing, (and good for them,) the sense that you could slip under someone else's skin and bring home a piece of their pain: a pain you look at, turning it over it in your mind like an object that ultimately reminds you of something.

I was 14 years old and I didn't know anything but we were pro-Palestinians and we were committed to hate Miami. A young woman takes her seat, I can see her from above because I am sitting behind the driver. I turn around to look at her. She's as gorgeous as she is different from all other women. She is black and has her hair up in the tightest bun I've ever seen. Her clean profile, the pearl earrings all the good girls used to wear at the time. Dark simple trousers, a little leather purse;

elegant. I turn back toward the driver and I lower my head. The man standing by her is shouting so much that I cannot help closing my eyes to calm my fear. I open my eyes just a bit to see my hands wet with my tears. I try to stand up and do something. I look at her again. I just watch her frightened face and I start crying so much that I can't see anything. The adult woman on on my side ignores me and her. Then the bus engine restarts; I clean my eyes but she's not there anymore. The man neither. I just hear the noise of the engine and the road below us.

I quickly got tired of being the first in my class. I felt disoriented by hate and I didn't identify with anything I saw beyond our doorstep. That was the community I owe my commitment to? They're the people to fight for? For them we must be "always the best ones"? The Guevarian rigor has made a huge leap from my mini-Soviet childhood to my 20's of reading and awareness. In between, as for everyone somehow, a confusing time of anger, music, underground culture and marijuana.

It was a frantic time in Italy as well. Soft dictators, censorship, laws presented by the Prime Minister to make the Prime Minister richer or safe from criminal trials; anti-mafia prosecutors attacked by the right wing for their investigations, the most prominent journalists kicked off national television for doing their job. Clowns on prime time and satire out of the door. Or in the streets, protesting, to say we are here, we'll always be.

It wasn't easy to keep up and I didn't pull it off any better than the others. In all that big mess, though, racism remained the most crushing defeat against the ultra-conservatives and corrupt political groups that ruled the country. It was, for me, the defeat living and breathing in my daily life, where Berlusconi and his associates' power to determine people's behavior was right in front of you; it was not on television, it happened in your neighbourhood, on the bus to school, in the streets. The words of hate, the colors of hate, the images of hate. Between the shouting and the insults it felt as if time had stopped, but it was just a hunch. The time was there, the present in which each of us had to choose what role to play in the history of those years.

That's why journalist Michele Santoro is so dear to me. And yes, also because he hung up on Berlusconi live on national television when so many others had the pricetag hanging off the jacket. But other than that, he always chose his words with care, whether they were heavy, effective words or the sweetness of an old, whispered song. In contrast to that was the uncanny ease with which people took part in hate and its trivial words. Antiracism in my heart has always compared to this levity the weight of every single word, sentence, or choice. I learned to cultivate the austerity of love.

FAROUK KASSAM KIDNAPPING IN AN ITALY WHICH NO LONGER EXISTS.

On 15th January 1992 in a fancy house in Porto Cervo, heart of luxury tourism in Sardegna, 7 year old Farouk Kassam was kidnapped by a local criminal group. A terrible game of chess began among kidnappers, Italian authority and the father of the child. It lasted 6 months , until the liberation of the hostage on 11th July 1992 in unclear circumstances.

Farouk's father, the owner of a hotel in the Costa Smeralda, was the nephew of the Visir of muslim imam and Iranian prince Karim Aga Khan. Fateh Kassam was a man of strong personality whose presence marked, for better or worse, the negotiations for his son's liberation. The Commander of the Operative Department of Oristano recalls the red car Fateh Kassam drove for dozens of kilometers back and forth in the impervious Sardegna's countryside looking for news of his son.

Absolutely not inclined to enter into immediate negotiation with the kidnappers, Fateh Kassam had harsh words even for those who were on his side. He considered the press just a useless nuisance which was slowing the search; the authorities also had a hard time with him, specially after the so called "block of the family assets", prescribed by the law in the attempt to stop the tragic chain of kidnappings so frequent in those years. His relationship with Graziano Mesina was also very troubled. Mesina was a local criminal who made a decisive contribution to the liberation of the child in exchange for a reduction of his sentence.

A strong man with a rough character, at some point Fateh would say when refusing to pay an overkill ransom: "If you are here to ask me for money I don't have, you can keep him. I am young, I can have other children". When the kidnappers led the investigators to find part of a child's earlobe, Fateh Kassam watched the picture of the child in silence, then he left without saying a single word. To the kidnappers he would say "Then, tear him apart so this is over".

During the press conference after the liberation of his son, despite the visible relief, he would have again harsh words for the journalists. Not only would he refuse to recognise that the press kept the public attention on the case, but he would plead with them not to do what they did with Farouk, accusing them of delaying his liberation.

In 1992 I was 13 years old. Every day the breaking news of every channel talked about the kidnapping. It was one of the last kidnappings of my childhood, among the many I remember in various parts of the country. The agonizing trickle of news, day after day. The liberation, or the sad incertitude about the destiny of the victim and the slow, inexorable end of the news about his kidnapping.

During the 6 months of Farouk Kassam's kidnapping Italy was united, with baited breath, waiting to know whether the child was alive and well; everyone wanted the child with the exotic name to come back home and the bad Italian criminals to be arrested.

After 3 months of kidnapping, the mother made an appeal to the women of the small town where the search focused: woman to woman, mother to mother, she asked them to do whatever they can to help bringing her son back. The citizens of Cagliari, a city in the South of Sardegna, replied to this moving appeal with a protest asking for the liberation of the child and sending an important message to the kidnappers: the local communities are on the side of the child's family and the State. Journalist Sergio Zavoli launched the idea of white sheets on the balconies in a sign of solidarity with the family. The "silent majority" in Italy can have such a different meaning than in every other part of the World. Such initiatives are always meaningful in Italy: public dissociation from local criminals, who in the past were considered almost as heroes, fighters for freedom against the oppression of the rule of the State, was a significant sign not only for Sardegna, at that time, but also for many other regions of South Italy. Still today in some areas such a choice is brave and even dangerous, if it's not shared by a community persuaded to change the course of its own history.

Farouk's little classmates with less exotic names remembered him everyday in a prayer, at the beginning of the lessons.

At the peak of the search the authorites would deploy 4000 men in a unprecedented operation in the history of the country.

That's what we did for Farouk Kassam. The-little-Farouk-Kassam. I don't remember a single journalist saying the word "muslim". He wasn't rich or poor, catholic or muslim, citizen or not. He was a child.

Italy today is not the same country anymore; a country of journalists who didn't make a sound when a muslim man with his foreign accent accused them of delaying the liberation of his son and, visibly annoyed, asked them never to do again what they did with his son's case. We did a lot for this family; we were supposed to and we knew it. And we rejoiced with them.

On 20th March 2019 a bus was hijacked. On the bus were 51 students and teachers. The hijacker was the driver who was acting in the name of his faith in ultra-radical Islam. He confiscated all the mobiles and threatened the kids with a knife. Ramy, a 13 year- old child from Morocco, managed to hide a mobile. With Adam, a 12 year- old child from Egypt, they are able to call the Carabinieri. The officers saved all the hostages and arrested the terrorist. When asked by a journalist, Ramy's father expressed the wish for his son to be granted Italian citizenship. Both Ramy and Adam were in fact foreigners, even if they were born in Italy, thanks to the "ius sanguinis" rule followed by Italian legislation. It's the "rule of the blood": you're Italian if your parents are Italian. Matteo Salvini, leader of the Northern League xenophobe party and Minister of the Interior Affairs, replied with contempt on Twitter (sic) that if Ramy wanted the citizenship he would have it when he was entitled to get elected to the Parliament and change the law. A Minister of the Republic was bullying a child who just saved 50 people from a terrorist. Eventually Ramy and Adam were granted Italian citizenship, not because they deserved to be recognised as heroes of the country they were born in, maybe waiting for the law to change; not because we were delighted by their action and their courage, but just because a Minister of the Republic didn't want look like a loser bullying a child. Not for too long.

We didn't do enough for these children, when they deserved it.

I am not so nostalgic. I live the present, fight for the future I want. But I am attached to the memory of Farouk Kassam. To what we were, we still could be.

THE BUBBLE

When I speak about racism in Veneto, many people assume I refer to my personal experience as a southerner living there. It's true that many of us suffered racism and discrimination in the North but to me, coming from the South meant essentially a certain amount of solitude and not much more than that. At the peak of our misfortune I was still very young, busy with my pride and games. I was a happy child and the contempt surrounding me could only scratch the surface of my joy. I hopped through my days with a glass full of mud and tadpoles, or a hammer stolen from my father's toolbox. It took me days to fix the tape recorder: the steel spikes didn't drive through the plastic. Turns out that there are a lot of purely ornamental pieces in a tape recorder. Done with the hammer, the tadpoles, plugs and stray cats, I usually started asking how much time was left before going to visit Grandma down in the South. From March onwards it was just a long wait for me; I spent my time plotting the death of my uncle Giulio, my mother's brother. Her fiance was my super favourite and I wanted her all for me. In addition, he ate a lot of the cakes and sweets Grandma used to make for me and my sister, not to mention that he was the favourite person of my mother, and the first one to take a shower after a day at the beach. All this was equally intolerable behaviour.

One day I stopped by the television. My parents were watching in a strange silence what was happening. My father didn't complain or comment. My mother looked frightened. I don't remmeber much more of a general anxiety. The journalist, a woman, was talking under footage of people destroying a painted wall and singing and hugging each others. I couldn't say from their faces whether it was positive or negative.

The fall of the Berlin Wall changed the history, the geography and the politics of the World; the social and economic expectations of the planet and its inhabitants, the distribution of the population and, eventually, our little lives.

One way or another, every country on Earth would find her new path in history, whether towards decolonisation and the affirmation of human rights or a renewed exploitation in the wake of a stronger, victorious capitalism now deprived of brakes (and shame). South Africa was the hope of a more equal and non-racist World, but in so many areas of the African continent the first years of the future global capitalism were more ruthless than ever before. Savage white men roamed the continent in search of the most corrupt in African politics and armies. Opaque figures were sent all around the African continent to put money in the hands of so-called rebels or mercenaries. Our capitalist economies started to feed on the horrors of African wars with a voracity unknown during the Cold War. In the desperate attempt to survive many African citizens embarked on dangerous journeys headed to the closest safe place: Europe.

Our stupidity was not comparable to what they had escaped from. This made (and still makes) them strong and weak at the same time.

Strong enough to survive and move on, endure whatever discrimination, and build a future for them and their loved ones.

Weak when it comes to find reasons to be engaged in the politics of their newly-adopted country. It took time and as far as I can see we're just now starting to see some direct engagement of African people in the unions or in politics. Still today it's difficult to imagine in Italy a civil rights movement as strong and outspoken as the North American one.

So they arrived. Young, determined. Suddenly my little pink cloud collided with reality. I can no longer just deliver kisses and think that means I am finished with fighting for justice. Antiracism becomes a daily, difficult choice. I was about 14 years old and not prepared to face violence. It left me shocked and frightened. It was just disturbing to constantly see people around me looking for someone else's suffering. It sounds strange, but you need to get used to something to counteract. In a state of fear and shock a reaction is difficult. From the girl with pearl earrings it took me time. It's like a sting, the first time you stand up and speak out, surrounded by annoyed strangers who ask you to shut up 'cause they are "just niggers, you idiot". This sense of the unknown, uncertainty. From there it's all downhill. Eventually, I got stronger, fearless. I got used to being looked at with suspicion or derision. I never really cared, but it got me nervous in the beginning. An antiracist act is seen as lack of tact, though. Bad taste. Chilling.

So the situation I was living in maybe helped me to be vocal about racial discrimination, but didn't improve my perception and knowledge of the Other.

Violence immediately creates distinct roles. There is the victim, the aggressor, and you. Looking at people belonging to a minority always as victims doesn't build your relationship with them , quite the opposite: <u>it destroys it.</u> Your eyes, used to to seeing those individuals frightened, attacked or even suffering, turn each of them into an infant, deprived not only of any defense but also their own character, their past, their background, everything.

I don't regret being there, though, taking a stand. It was right to let victims know they aren't alone; right to let racists know they can't get away with what they say everytime. Right for me, to stay who I am. Because your history defines who you are and that is primarily your public choices, including what you decide to do when facing the community around you which will support, or will judge and isolate you. You have no control over what comes after your action, but you are willing to take the risk because you think it's worth it. Your story is the responsibility you take. If you don't risk anything you're a child playing in the backyard.

After I arrived in England, I found myself constantly checking out what was happening to black people around me. I realized then how sick racism made me It rendered me intoxicated and far removed from a healthy relationship with the Other .

Like a child I started to enjoy the company of minority people. Their voices, their opinions, their tastes in food, their laughter, their feelings. They're strange, very normal, fun, weirdos. Slowly, the victim becomes a person and the child an old girl.

It just stings sometimes to be living in my English-speaking bubble. As soon as the plane lands in Italy I am back in that space of my mind where most of the time the color of your skin determines your job, economic situation, the attitude people have towards you. And I have to choose whether to be complicit in another vicious comment or act accordingly and go away again. And then, again - and again.

THIS IS THE NIGHT

Racism and city buses are forever connected in our collective memory to the movement for the end of racial segregation and civil rights in the United States. When I thought about that I stood still, my head slightly swinging and my eyes lost, staring at a fixed point. It happens to me when I lose track of time and space. I don't know where I am or for how long I've been there. I am lost in my own thoughts.

The idea hit me and left me dizzy, confused by its simplicity. For all my life, since I was 12 and started going to school by bus alone, that had been my personal nightmarish place. The mobile lair where the very worse always happened. Every day, every trip, every time a black person got on the bus.

It had all started on the buses and there, somehow, continued.

In the early '90s in Italy the eternally disappointed men and women with fake lives and minds broken by the frustration of not getting what they never fought for threw themselves beyond redemption on their nice bowl of racism like hungry dogs.

The number of black people was continually increasing . War after extermination after genocide after famine, until the end of the communist dream and the Soviet nightmare allowed them to do the only thing anybody would have done: run away towards safer places.

Anybody who knows anything about war, through study or personal experience, aknowledges that the most dangerous person after a war is the victim.

Surviving the horror of war, the victim is a witness asking for justice and restoration. Their very existence is an indictment, a memory capable of being shared. So after witnessing war and its horrors, ethnic cleansing and discrimination, survivors are subject to persecutions and forced to move away from their lands. War criminals trying to get away with their crimes are the main reasons many people in Kosovo fled abroad after the war and are, even after decades, afraid to come back and risk meeting their persecutors in the streets. This is what happens in the case of civil war, but the situation is not much different when it comes to the extermination wars in Africa. Those last ones, apparently waged only by local subjects but guided in fact by the interest of foreign economic powers, are wars for the control of economic resources.

In those wars a "strategy" often used as war weapon is rape. On a large scale, rape spreads HIV and other venereal diseases, destroys families by alienating women from fathers, husbands and sons. It cuts them off from a community that, losing them, falls apart. A community shocked and divided is fragile, unable to react while around them rebels in name only and corrupted armed servants of western capitalism take control of territory to export natural resources without leaving anything for the locals (such as taxation, fair work conditions or salaries, infrastructures). The children working in the mines of Coltan for next to nothing are the first link of the chain ending up in our glossy down-town shops: the Western slavers of the African night.

The eyes of the victims of all those horrors are looking at us, across the road or from the window of a bus. We don't want their eyes on us. They don't have to reveal the road they travelled; a trail of blood and death beginning in the small villages they come from and ending in our homes, our mobiles, our jewellery. We are the last link of this macabre chain while those who are only guilty of innocence are Them, the immigrants.

For this reason at least racism is vital for the actual liberal system. Not only is a powerful way to deflect our attention from the criminal roots of our economic system, but it's essential for the very existence of capitalism. Liberals need to sneak into our minds the notion that racism is justifiable and justified by an economic system we can't change. We don't want to change it. We can't even believe that it could change.

Today it seems all much more complicated than it really is. Some of us, incapable of just conceiving a victory of people against turbo-capitalism's oppression and its necessary forms of exploitation, looked for shorter alternatives and routes. A road chosen to embrace a life in which there's no difference between existing and appearance. It's not only youngsters who are lost in this world of frivolities disguised as sacred liberties. Many people live hidden behind a paper activism, behind the idea that writing on Twitter about something equates to denouncing it publicly. It's a huge illusion, useful just to winkle out apathy. Unfortunately for those rag soldiers the old battles for rights must be fought always the same way: collectively in the streets we live, not as sum of individuals on the web where we hide. Politicians know this very well, so they don't take the battles seriously. They know thousands of little revenges don't make justice for the whole of us. Justice is an ideal we achieve walking the path together, which means, in our societies, just one thing: Justice can only reach our lives through institutions. In the institutions our rights come to life and society takes charge of what happened to us, spending money for us investigating, convening a trial, punishing the culprits. Justice is society that joins our pain and, somehow, returns what was taken.

Believing those soft protests are going to work demonstrates an optimism that's killing all of us. It's a hideous and deceitful attitude: denouncing unjustices in the World and saying "but one day it will change". When? Thanks to what change in our lives? What exactly will bring us to the path of justice and equality? Leftist liberals usually reply with apodictic as much as generic statements. My favourites are things like "I strongly believe in the ability of women to change the World". I happen to believe women <u>could</u> change the World but it's a completely meaningless statement, not only because women don't hold the power to do so. Also, the gender of the individuals perpetuating the manifold capitalist unjustices is irrelevant. Capitalism need slaves and, therefore, racism, and that's equally true for the men and women profiting from this system. Man or woman, their lifestyles depend on the system's leakage. The vast majority of us live on the other side, women and men, waiting for a change that nobody with a minimum of decision-making power wants to give us. In the Third World citizens don't have rights and the imperative is preventing them from claiming any. In the First World, with the slow but inexorable deterioration of the conditions of the working class, the keyword is "distraction", and today with social media it is not even difficult. We entertain ourselves becoming soft-porn actresses on Instagram, professional haters, or influencers, a word that stands for "cyber-clerk selling stuff to people using her house as fitting room".

In one way or another, questions are avoided and revolutions just a memory. While racism infuriates in a way that never happened after World War II, the liberal hypocrisy still pretends to believe that politics can change the path of something politicians lost control of long ago.

Capitalism, which regulates itself only in liberal fairy tales, looks for profit at the expense of everything and primarily everyone. Rights are impediments; racism is exploitation of blacks, distraction of whites. The acquisition of technology in our daily life changed everything and nothing. The way we do things changed forever but what we do exactly? Do we have more rights? More time to enjoy the only life we are given thanks to technology? Did the quality of life of the masses improve? Did the fact we are able to see literally everything happening in real time all over the World change the pattern of our capitalism in Africa? Technology may be (in the future?) an instrument for change; social media, which are today a huge part of the web, are nothing more than a market. With a disturbing turn from post-feminism to pre-universal adult suffrage, young women use social network to make soft-porn videos to sell clothes, make-up and themselves to rich men who don't need much more from them than what they can see on their Instagram profile. Did the technology make any kind of contribution to the fight against racism? We can watch people drown in real time in the Mediterranean Sea; we saw a little girl crying, desperate to see her parents again at the border of the USA with Mexico. We know precisely how people live in the Gaza Strip, we became aware of the condition of Syrian refugees in Greece or Italy.

It's precisely in the face of those tragedies that far right parties won all over in Europe and Trump won the presidency in the USA. In this context, hate is working better than ever as a machine generating political consent. I assume the impoverishment of the working class in the First World countries is speaking to poor white people that can't find anything better than the short-term strategy of racism to save themselves from a destiny which is so horribly close to them. It's the secret awareness that the well-known downward trend of capitalism as depicted by neo-Marxists is an actual reality and the only answer possible is renewing hate, reviving discrimination, in a worrying return to the past that was hardly predictable only few years ago. Yet all the while the protest is left in the hands of liberals; it's no coincidence that liberals adore specific protests. The women on one side, the blacks on the other with all the debate about the contribution feminism (or just women?) made to white supremacism. The environmentalists on another corner, the gays on the other. No matter how many people you bring onto the streets, which in the digital era is already a victory: until the protest is just one for Justice against the system, none of these initiatives is going to be seen as a danger to those who discriminate, or destroy the environment or segregate minorities.

But how important is racism for the political and economic forces willing to perpetuate the capitalist system? It's crucial.

The example of Stephen Miller as an advisor to President Donald Trump may be enlightening. Also known as "the quiet extremist", in November 2019 Stephen Miller was involved in a scandal revealed by a series of emails sent by Miller to far-right website 'Breitbart' writer Katie McHugh. Based on a report of by the Southern Poverty Law Center (SPLC) which revealed the email's content, 80% of the approximately 900 emails concerned immigration-related issues. Despite denying any link with the white supremacist movement , Miller was discussing with McHugh the best way to align the News section of Breitbart's website to conspiracy theories typical of the far-right nationalists in order to support the presidential campaign of Donald Trump. From the correspondence we also discover that the inspiration for the website has been J. Simpson's book "The red-green axis: Refugee, Immigration and the agenda to erase America". The author states that welcoming refugees is part of a global plan to erase American white sovereignty and culture.

Miller, whose poor image as a public figure is well-known thanks to an unfortunate interview for CNN, is responsible for the implementation of Trump's anti-immigration agenda. When the emails became public knowledge, a hundred members of the Congress, dozens of civil rights activist groups and many others asked the President to fire him or ask for his resignation. During the Presidency with the highest number of officers fired in American history, with a President who didn't hesitate to abandon his men "under the attack" of press or judiciary (as happened, for example, to Rudy Giuliani), the only 'untouchable' was Stephen Miller. Donald Trump didn't fight as much for Steve Bannon, the most notorious (and internationally-known) advisor he'd had during his campaign, but Miller's position was never in jeopardy even after a scandal that connected him directly to the white supremacists. Steve Bannon, the man of slogans and propaganda, wasn't essential. The man who put in place the administrative adjustment to actually bring the US administration into line with white supremacism was untouchable. That's how important racism is for a conservative vision of a capitalist economy. It reminds me of the fundamental place anti-semitism had in Nazi Germany. Every now and then mankind seems to underestimate the power of racism to unify people under the same flag. I, myself, am a neo-marxist. I am waiting for all those white supremacists to see the day when, even in their first world, capitalism will need more victims. Ownership of territory and water granted to white people instead of a native reservation; low qualified workers impossible to find in other vanished minorities will be found elsewhere. They want slaves, and the condition of employees of a relatively new big company such as Amazon doesn't tell us any different. But for now, poor useless racists, enjoy your superiority, embrace impunity. Your chains to a life of slavery are waiting for you right around the corner, along with the bullet they will fire at your head at the first sign of rebellion. Or maybe another left-wing liberals' glamorous virtual protest against racism will convince you that things will change. Tomorrow.

 I was raised in a slightly different way. Once I asked my parents what they thought about some ideas circulating at school about Che Guevara being a murderer, because revolution is, obviously, a violent action against the system. My mother, irritated, replied: if you want to do a revolution you get the shotgun and you kill people. Otherwise you stay home and watch TV.

I never saw myself with a shotgun. And I did understand that behind my mother's statement there was also the idea that you should not talk about things for which you don't take responsibility. It just bothers me so much that an armed rebellion against all the madness we live in (and for) is a deviant terrorist idea whereas hundreds of armed Nazis shooting at innocents protesters are allowed to do so, or lynching and executing an unarmed man jogging doesn't have terrible consequences. A woman executed while sleeping in her bed is not a big deal. Violence can be normalized if illegally used against minorities but it's called terrorism if illegally used against inequality. The difference? The value those acts of racism have for capitalism; the danger represented by people just trying to reach a more equal, antiracist World.

HERE AND THERE

Increasingly often we read shocking news from the USA about terrifying episodes of racism which are difficult to delete from the mind. Some episodes are even hard to believe, like the murder of Breonna Taylor sleeping in her house.

Today, we know about those innocent lives who were taken away from their loved ones because of the colour of their skin. That's one of the biggest achievements of the Black Lives Matter movement, born in 2013 following the pointless murder of the teenage Trayvon Martin by supremacist George Zimmerman, who was later acquitted by an all-white jury.

I knew about discrimination and racism in the USA. I knew their history enough not to be surprised by their profound ignorance and disregard for other people's lives. I have to admit I didn't expect the numbers, the intensity of the constant oppression and violence in the streets, the horrific pleasure they take in posing for pictures and becoming local stars thanks to their crimes, and the pride they take in those crimes.

It occurs to me that still in 2020 those protestant settler cultures can't free themselves from their original sin: that of being the product of the ethnic cleansing of the territory they occupied.

However, it's a degree of violence that, here in Europe, we inflicted on others but didn't experience in our own streets. There is no difference in terms of responsibilities between Italians sending innocent Jewish citizens to death in Poland and protestant settlers exterminating native Americans and enslaving people from Africa. There is a huge difference in what the population experienced and internalized of its own culture, in the habits that make the life people are used to. Indifference on one side, cruelty on the other. Italian moral corruption and North American white-supremacism. It really adds up.

As I said, Italy knows violence and has practised it widely. And we shoud always praise Moni Ovadia and his fight (one of his many) against the false and pathetic cliche of "Italiani brava gente" (Italian good people).

It may be interesting to compare the differences between these two countries to look for insights or hints for a change.

It's quite clear that the worse violence has always been seen in places and times of history when the law allowed it.

In Italy, during fascism, with the Law of the Race we joined the Germans on the path that led us all to the horror of the extermination of six million innocents Jews and about two million of other people including Romani communities, homosexuals, and political opponents.

In the United States racism has always been an integral part of the system, and formally so until the end of segregation. But, while the history of a country and its laws have a great influence on society, at the same time it's not enough to justify the situation black people still endure today.

An effective change in the actual lives of many African-American citizens would need an authentic political commitment to bring into the community not only the change promised by the end of segregation and the Civil Rights Act of 1964, but also a radical step-change within their institutions: a judge who applied the Jim Crow laws up to the day before their abolition will surely find a different way to get the same results and so please the racists who voted for him; a judge can surely bypass a law (ask a lawyer).

The very same lack of an essential change of the institutions occurred in Italy, although with different consequences, more related to corruption in national politics and, at least in human terms, less tragic. After the end of fascism, as requested by the Americans, all the individuals who had political and institutional responsibilities during fascism weren't removed, but remained within the new Italian Republic administration. This is one of the many reasons why the CIA, in the search of allies for its subversive and antidemocratic plans in Europe during the Cold War, always found reachable counterparts within Italian institutions, but that's another story.

Today, our situation has changed, somewhat. Racism in Italy is a complicated interweaving of various indecencies: political, moral corruption, indifference towards the other's destiny, lives soaked in comfortable lies, social frustration due to economic issues, greed, pettiness.

But still, we didn't get rid of the fascist culture of the scapegoat, the race who'll get the blame for everything. We also allowed the degrading addition of a pathetic, false middle-class respectability that apparently allows someone to claim they're not racist while still saying the worst things I have ever had to listen to. Casually – dressed human garbage. Not to mention that Italy is full of village idiots dreaming of becoming the Duce, with a special concentration in the North-East of the country.

All this occurs, in Italy, within our society and politics.

Nevertheless, the Constitution of the Republic protects our disgraced country.

Our Constitution was written after World War II and is one of the most clear constitutions when it comes to civil, political, union and especially human rights.

The judiciary system is intended to send back to the Constitutional Court any issue of conflict between a law and the Constitution. So, if a discriminatory act occurs and the law applicable to the case doesn't protect the human rights violated or in fact doesn't punish the crime, or not enough, the issue is sent to the Court that can abolish the law. The Parliament is thereby obligated to change the law to be consistent with the constitutional principle in question, or even this second version will be repealed.

In addition, this system is secured by the independence of the judiciary by the other powers of the State, thanks to a self- governance body called Consiglio Superiore della Magistratura, which is solely responsible for positions assignment, promotions and, probably more importantly, punitive measures.

So, in Italy, at least our Constitution protects us with hard work but never misses a step. Immediately after fascism the judiciary experienced a period of some sort of continuity, but during the decades a process of democratisation started: the old judges retired and the judiciary system, independent of politics, selected new judges only based on their knowledge of the republican laws based on the new Constitution, instead of their political opinions or acquaintances. So just the best ones became part of the system, rich and poor, conservatives and liberals, from north and south: a compact group of judges having as sole point of reference the republican law and the Constitution was thus formed. As a result, anyone who walks into court in Italy as victim of discrimination and can prove it is very unlikely to lose.

So, despite the human scum which reaches the Parliament straight from the worst human cesspool of the country, the judiciary saves us from falling prey to that fascist violence Italy knows very well.

In the Unites States The American Constitution dates back to 1787. All rights and liberties expressed in it refer to white citizens. Slavery was not even at its end when the Constitution was written; it ended in 1865 (!!) with the inclusion (!!) of the XIII Amendment to the original version of the constitution.

African-Americans are, still today, an amendment in

their own country.

The United States legally discriminated against them until the 1960s, when segregation's institutions and laws were dismantled, slowly and not easily (little-known but sad is the story of the end of segregated public swimming pools in the USA)

What can we say about racism in America? A few, but hopefully meaningful, things.

It's a story of institutions and laws: institutionalized pervasive racism, drawn by capillary action into every public and private sector of life.

Institutions, especially if they last for so long, shape their community.

The beautiful, deserving fight of African-Americans did immensely for Usa black community. Still, face of the senseless murders of innocents that don't even spare little children, it seems to have just scratched the surface of a discrimination which is an all-present poison: a poison white people are fed since their childhood, a poison that seems to have become essential to their way of life.

They have someone to hate when things go wrong, someone to exploit when things go well, a relief valve for their frustration. It's quite difficult to think that people whose ignorance is rated today so low in the chain leading to the definition of humanity could give all this up. One proof thereof is the shocking lynching and murder of the young Ahmaud Arbery, as well as the ugly cases of assassinations in cold blood of young African-Americans (last but not least a young woman, a medical worker killed by Louisville police officers while sleeping in her bed), occurring on daily basis in the Unites States.

To sum up, if I had to define the big difference between American and Italian racism I would cite the institutionalisation of hate and the lack, in the United States, of a primary and fundamental political will to erase that hate.

In the Unites States, probably the country with the most engaged, self conscious black community in the West World, the judiciary hasn't changed that much. A judge elected in the same way as politicians, who built his career on the back of black people living in his jurisdiction, is very unlikely to change his policy and beliefs overnight. That would mean betraying the many racist citizens who voted for him exactly because he assured them respectand to follow with his decisions their same policies and beliefs and, primarily, their racism. Racists elect racists and if you don't respect your commitment, they will vote for someone else. You will lose your job, your position, your place in a community that trusted you to be one of them.

However, more than anything else there is, in my opinion, a constitutional problem. A judge would have to adhere to the Constitution if it changed, becoming a stronghold of liberty and equality for all citizens, not just all white citizens.

But if the American Constitution doesn't change, if national politics leaves black people being an unpleasant additional amendment and so, somehow, not essential, why should a simple local judge act any better than this?

PROTEST AND... PROTEST?

Racism is a problem concerning justice and society. In the United States in particular the involvement of the democratic institution in systematic discrimination against and persecution of black people is a major problem and that's the reason why the main requests of the Black Lives Matter movement are the end of police brutality, illegal and unjust detention, and discrimination within the justice system towards them. Their struggle is a struggle for justice.

There is, apparently, another fight for justice born in recent years in the United States; the MeToo movement. This movement was born following the Ronan Farrow scoop about the many sex-related crimes of Hollywood producer Harvey Weinstein and the subsequent speech of Asia Argento denouncing the intolerable condition of the women in show business. I do believe Miss Argento's accusations and I admire the courage of a woman who didn't know what was about to happen after speaking out but decided to act without any kind of guarantee or safety parachute. She was great. But the consequences were not in her hands and I must say I didn't see any more courage and strength in what happened next.

The difference between those two movements are interesting and underline the meaning institutions have in our lives and why is so important to believe in them and entrust to them our request for justice.

When it comes to discrimination against black people in the United States, the amount of evidence concerning every single crime committed is usually huge. Actually, the real issue is that despite the irrefutable proof of a crime committed against a black person, the culprits often get away with it. On the other side, over the years too many black men were sentenced and convicted; nevertheless, several cases are still surrounded by so many doubts that it's difficult to understand the reasons why they were arrested in the first place apart from than the colour of their skin.

For these reasons Black Lives Matter is a political movement, aiming to change how institutions act towards black people; protesters claim their right to be equally treated when they face justice, when they are questioned by police. They ask the authorities to respect their fundamental rights, to respect the law.

Of course, it's a long path, but it's the only one that really matters: the long, uphill climb that will lead to the recognition of an equal, just treatment for all Black people once and forever.

Except for few notorious cases like the Bill Cosby trial, when it comes to MeToo movement, there are no people who are undoubtedly victims of a crime demanding justice. The alleged victims take "justice" into their own hands and act. No institutions need be involved, no matters of evidence. It's a story told by the lone voice of the person who claims to be the victim of crime.

There is a huge misunderstanding here, concerning the very same concept of justice.

When, in the past, feminists and all decent persons used to say "believe women", they didn't mean "believe women when, comfortably lying in their bed, make accusations no authority never investigated without any other evidence than their own version of the facts". That is not 'believing women': that is historically called a 'witch-hunt.'

What those brave women and men meant was that, when a woman addresses the justice system asking for justice, she must not be ignored. The justice system must investigate the allegations, look for the truth, and give female victims of sexual abuse the justice they deserve.

And I personally think it's very significant that the vast majority of those social network accusations are not brought in front of a judge, where impartial authorities may be able to establish what happened and at least try to punish the culprit.

The main objection is that the system is not impartial.

I would reply that Twitter in not exactly the solution for a broken justice system. Or do some of those women think the relatives of George Floyd or little Tamir Rice can actually find justice shouting their outrage and pain on social media?

But there is an even more relevant reply: the same idea of fighting for justice is about trying to change the system and make it impartial where is not, because justice is what our community recognises as our right as members of that community.

Justice is what you ask (and deserve) from the system, not something you can reach just flaunting your (genuine.. or not?) pain on Twitter.

For these reasons the MeToo movement won't benefit women around the World in any way. Every accusation may destroy a career (and, let's not forget, a family), but the result is just those 15 minutes of fame for the victim. They may be even a real victim, but a victim who preferred vengeance to justice. The individual satisfaction instead of justice through the institutions, the only justice that sets a precedent and represents an actual advancement for all women.

SWEET, WHITE SLEEPING BEAUTY

I have to admit I am stunned by the blatant dishonesty of some white Americans and white American women in particular in the face of the African-American citizens demanding justice in the wake of the Black Lives Matter movement.

White women are simply brazen and convinced that, while black people are in the streets fighting against the result of centuries of discrimination, they can give us, a surreal and naive image of themselves. Although it may seem pathetic, they are all over the web and social media asking silly questions like "what can I do to help", or trying to figure out what kind of white privileges they were enjoying, or pretending they acknowledge today the pervasiveness of discrimination against black people in their very own country. It's an easy way to look friendly now, when it's highly convenient to do so; trying to make people think that, at the end of the day, they have always been there ready to help while enjoying their white-privileged lives without guilt.

But this image belongs to the slippery world of communication in the internet era. Today, the people who read our words can be so distant from the reality we describe that being deceitful while pretending to be supportive is very easy. So today we have this cute little army of white women willing to acknowledge their white privileges, willing to help.

Unfortunately for this heavenly picture, black people are hitting the streets to fight against injustice that white people, included white women, aren't able to just figure out. They are involved in it.

I wonder if all these whining women have ever been in

a post office; in the traffic, in line at the bank, if they have spent a day working with other people one day in their whole lives, if they've ever been in a restaurant or a bookshop, or if they've ever bought a fashion magazine.

The idea instilled in Karen's mind that she can get a black man arrested and, who cares, possibly killed for the sake of her unleashed dog is not a personal belief of a disturbed woman. It's rather the product of the deep acknowledgement of the general consent she senses around her when she acts like that. She recognises the silence around her: it's the very same silence she granted to another woman, the tacit consent she claims as her right when she looks clearly in front of the camera, unconcerned; with the nerve of someone who knows that, as a white woman, she's never alone.

But back to you, Sleeping Beauty. Having gone through the difficult times of the Civil Rights Movement, outrage and protest throughout the years, you know the drill today. It's all about trying to save face and hold tight until the storm has passed.

It reminds me a proverb we use in Italy to describe the strategy the Sicilian mafia adopt in time of troubles. "Bend over, reed, for the flood is coming". When the attention of authorities and public opinion rises, they try to become invisibles keeping a low profile and waiting for the "flood" to pass. They adapt to survive for the sole aim of coming back to 'normal' as soon as the attention subsides.

I am sure there are a lot of white people in the USA who were waiting for this protest to publicly express their dissent with how North American society treats their black friends, wives, sons or just fellow citizens. I don't doubt the authenticity of their beliefs and their commitment and part of my hope comes from their engagement in the current protests because I think it's so important to send the USA's politicians the clear message that a more equal country is a concern for all society, not just black people.

Nevertheless, many statements I've been reading coming from white women on the subject are preposterous and so terribly disingenuous that I don't even know how someone can work up the courage to border on ridicule so manifestly.

Time is the big issue here. Centuries of history. Decades of your life.

You didn't notice. You didn't know the extent of the problem. Never happened in front of you. You never had a single chance to say something, to act. Really?

I don't even bother to dispute what you say. I am not going to insult my intelligence.

I am not pretending your words are sincere.

For your entire life you didn't care and let's be very honest: there is just one thing that makes this protest different from the previous ones: social media. Without social media no one would have been able to read your excuses, or better, to know that you didn't provide any explanation about how you address the issue of racism against black people. Without social media you wouldn't have bothered to ask "what can I do", as you didn't do in the past. As you didn't do in the '90s during Los Angeles protests; as you didn't do when Trayvon Martin was killed. Or Zimmerman acquitted.

You had an entire life to know better, to say something, to expose and denounce, to do what you could. You didn't. The destiny, life, struggle and suffering of black men, women, children, have never been enough to make you postpone the smallest of your daily undertakings.

When anti-racist educator Jane Elliott asked if someone would have exchanged his life with the life of a black person, no one accepted. Would you? I really don't think so, Sleeping Beauty.

Sure, perfect innocence is not required. We all can change, we all can do better. After all anti-racism is a path, rather than a personal quality acquired once and forever.

Now is the right time. I like to think the best course of

action is, first of all, to face reality, and accept that the length of your criminal indifference is so outrageous that no one can seriously doubt the right black people have to be sick of your excuses and apologies.

This prostration, the profound sense that you should have done so much more to prevent the situation from deteriorating as it did, is a real blessing for Black Lives Matter. It will help protestors to detect your intentions, to see through your gentle, very late words.

And keep fighting as much as they can, for as long as they need.

In solidarity

BULL TRUMP AND THE DAY AFTER TOMORROW

In 1963, after viewing television reports of the water-hose and police-dogs episodes, President John Kennedy said: "The civil rights movement should thank God for Bull Connor. He helped it as much as Abraham Lincoln."

Theophilus Eugene "Bull" Connor was a local politician in Birmingham, Alabama, during the Civil Rights Movement protests. In the State where Martin Luther King Jr. lived and preached, Bull Connor was in charge of the supervision of the local police department. His strong opposition to the Civil Rights Movement from within the Birmingham city council led to the shocking images of peaceful protesters besieged by police officers with water hoses and attack dogs. Those were the reports President Kennedy referred to in his famous quote, understanding that those disturbing images were about to spark outrage and, in doing so, consolidate the support for the Movement, both inside and outside the United States.

The current disgrace is that the man who until recently was playing the very same role as Bull Connor was the President of the United States. He was vastly more powerful than his "predecessor"; he could oppose the ongoing protests with so many institutional instruments that we really had to fear that his ignorance and ineptitude could leave more blood on the streets than a democracy can endure without becoming a full-blown dictatorship. That's one more reason why the peaceful attitude of the vast majority of the protesters is crucial to achieve the aims of justice and prevent the situation from escalating, giving any President an excuse for the political and social repression of the protest.

Trump was, legitimately, the catalyst of our indignation. But, in my mind, he's also the symbol of despair of an ending world, or at least this is my hope.

Since the raise of the environmentalist protest FridayForFuture we all saw how incredible is the good which young and committed people can do together and with the help of social media.

When the protests started in the US I saw a parallel between the two protests.

Not only because, as neo-Marxists clearly explained since the 90's, when we respect the environment we end up respecting human rights.

I saw how both these ideas have spread like wildfire, like almost nothing before.

It reminds me Berkley and the protests of the 1970's, which were the last ones that changed the World from end to end.

Is the bright destiny of this protest to eventually give Black people the better, more righteous World they deserve??

I don't know, and it's so strange not being there, not being young anymore. Italy had its part in the fight, its history of protest in the name of a freedom we still miss today. And that's my point.

Because my heart and my prayers are with the protesters; not just for my deep solidarity with the cause of justice and equality but also for as an Italian, I had a little taste of your future.

In 1994 Berlusconi achieved power. He was, like Trump, one of the richest men in the World. An entrepreneur, like Trump: a man who used his public powers to grow his business; a racist who divided and corrupted a whole country; a liar who used his influence on the media to manipulate the information given to the citizens, discrediting every journalist who tried to ask simple questions.

Some important truths saw the light thanks to journalists, intellectuals, and writers. They are my personal heroes, they lost so much for us. Lions roaring in the battle, alone against armies of crooked politicians and servile journalists.

Even so, my memories don't erase the final truth: we lost the battle. And I wish I could show you, young Black people, the Italy we live in today.

It's a country lost in its hate for Black people and immigrants. Every time this hate reaches the news, I am more and more disgusted by the meanness of my very own people.

A country lost in a blood-soaked tie of national politics with organized crime, where the corruption of minds and public powers is beyond redemption.

Fight, brothers, and may your God be with you.

In solidarity

ANOTHER REBEL DAY

I was walking as if I was in a hurry. When I realized it, I tried to slacken my pace, breathe and look around. The plaza was wet from a drizzling rain, the October's wet damp cold. I heard a few distant voices and felt that weird feeling of loss you experience when something which you thought was going fine falls apart and you're far from home. It's a slight but perceivable dizziness, not knowing what to do to change what didn't work. This feeling was exacerbated by the fact that I was on holidays and didn't have any plans. Nothing to do but waste my time going around town. The day I realized that, thank God, Padova was no longer home for me.

I turn my gaze towards the centre of the Plaza and I glimpse the usual booth of some political party collecting signatures. I wonder who 's going to be be kicked out this time. In this town most of the times there's someone to chase away. "Signatures collection" is a very benign expression, but this is the jaded inconsistency of the town. Trans-gender people are dilettantes: the champions of disguise don't aspire to expensive sex change operations; they evade any more than the minimum needed involuntary psych commitment.

I see the Northern League flag and suddenly I find myself almost running in the opposite direction. I reach the other side of the Plaza, and stop for a moment. A passer-by crosses before my sad eyes, already lost in the next 15 minutes of my life. He'd be wondering what's wrong with me but I never had the strength to go beyond my personal efforts and proselytize, even for such a sacred cause. You can't find the right words if you can't explain the justice of a cause to yourself in the first place but just feel it, furiously flowing in your veins. If only you too, passer-by, would feel it in your veins.

I don't say a word, I bite my lips and hold back a pissed-off, tiresome grimace.. I breath in deeply and throw myself into the next 15 minutes. I know them well, I know the words. My words, their words. I know how this story ends: with me on one side of a fence I was not the only one able to see, once; everybody else, for different reasons, on the other side. There is just a moment, of those 15 minutes, that still gives me some gratification. Their amazed faces when they realized derision doesn't work with me. Insults didn't bother them too much, but that little moment, the very instant they look me straight in the eyes with that demented laugh on their sordid faces but they soon realize I don't laugh, I don't step back, I don't feel awkward. That's the secret moment between me and them, the moment I win: I already won. If someone else could see it, he would notice that that's the moment they start shouting, to see if they scare me. Then they just lose it. The blonde lady with her fancy purse shouts coarsely but with no conviction, the elder beast wags her finger towards me. Men start yelling incoherent slogans and I kindly cherish that moment of strength which will be my sole companion for the coming days. I put it in my pocket and my voice, broken with shame and outrage, exposes them and I point at them. After the decision of some of the city councils of the Region to take food out of immigrant children's mouth in the schools, they feel they're going to have a very easy ride now. They never expect to be questioned, to hear the simple truth like that, with no warning, in public. I called Northern League people "Nazi, anti-Semites, racists". Unthinkable.

While sipping my beloved little post-lunch coffee in the historic Caffe' Cavour I can see all this inconceivability shaping up around me. Two ugly mugs who were in the Plaza under the red and yellow flag followed me . They shoot around me nervously with their phones glued to their ears.

I smile. They look like patients escaped from a psychiatric ward who think they're CIA agents on duty. The dangerous subversive is sending a text message to her friend Eleonora. She is going to take a little walk in the city centre again, in case the idea that she is afraid and going to run away before facing her serious responsibility could occur to them. She is going back home then, to take a little nap before dinner.

I am gathering my things from the table while a few other customers around me notice something's wrong. You should have the right to a coffee at Caffe' Cavour after giving compelling evidence of antiracism activity for at least 5 minutes per day. I can see them, the ladies in their Hermes shawls with the labradoodle queuing with the phone in one hand " — Just caught them in Piazza delle Erbe, Almost 6 minutes! — Would you show me the video, please? — Here. — Just a second.. recorded. Thank you, here's your receipt".

And you, drinking your not-hard-to-get coffee, freed from fatigue and frustration by a rebellion you don't want to end, don't ask me anything.

I come back home, I drop my purse and slowly lay down on the bed. I enjoy that little moment for myself. To rest a minute and stop the time, looking at it and tell myself "remember it was worth it" despite all it was about to happen. Because you know it, you saw it day by day for years. That is how the silence actual works: whether you break it or you share it.

REMEMBERING NERUDA

And I realise that spitting on the face of a local politician is not universally condemned as is my unexplicable lack of democratic spirit, when it comes to racism and other (unconstitutional) amenities.

Simply: I've broken the silence. One of the police officers in command at the Police Departement will tell me so, even indirectly. A strange encounter. The officer in command barely let me reply to his questions, when he arrived after half an hour of chatting with the police officer who picked me up at home. But with him, I can't finish a single sentence, except the ritual ones about England, life abroad, the youth leaving the country and the better opportunities. He's kind, calm. He's home. I don't know whether to start trying to explain my actions. I am totally at ease, so not in my natural habitat of verbal violence and hostility which rules in town, over these walls. He doesn't accuse me of things I didn't do. He doesn't abuse me, it's quite confusing but nothing gives me reason to shoot so my brain slowly reaches the holster and puts on the safety catch. I try to understand what's going to happen but they just need my signature on a paper, a mild administrative sanction: "A warning", they call it.

The high officer is very kind but he wants me to know that he has the information he needs, and his opinion on the subject. A tiny little drop of poison in an ocean of clean water.

- So I've heard that you're leaving tonight.

No one knows I am leaving tonight except my parents and my sister. Not even my dearest friend, the only person I still hang out with in town. Probably my father had told them when they came home to pick me up, before calling me Therefore he doesn't chat about it. He told me like he wants my reaction, or to let me know his reaction. I look at him weirded-out, he maybe thinks I wanted to hide it. But the reason that pushed me to pay for the second ticket is simple and crude.

- Yes, I am leaving. I have the old return ticket but I think I'll leave tonight. Journalists are calling home, coming into the neighbourhood and.. my sister delivered a child two weeks ago and she needs quiet.

- Of course, I understand.

- Yeah...

Yeah. My sister, in the middle of her phase "The children of men", the only woman who ever delivered on the planet, is happy but tired. She had a C-section and she's just recovered. I was never able to communicate properly with her and she clearly doesn't want me home. She didn't want me before my little clash with the Northern League in the city center, even less now after what I did.

But this high officer at least tells me something new. No one is perfect. He explains to me why they decide to sanction my action, even though with just a warning. He tells me "It's been years since years something like that happened". I record the information and keep listening to him. I can't think about it because I am focused on swimming towards the end of this pool full of baffling, police peacefulness.

While two police officers take me back home to avoid the journalists, I look around me and I see the squares and the streets we used to fill against what we thought was the personification of evil. I believed then no-one was worse than Berlusconi and his xenophobe friends of the Northern League, I was sure that after him the Northern League would have run out of allies and would crawl back into the sewer where they came from. I guess I hoped the fight wouldn't have been longer than my youth and I could live happily ever after. It was so comforting to think that the evil was just Berlusconi, forgetting the dregs around him. In the Parliament, in the streets. Following him, voting him, paid by him, corrupted by him. The very worst fed on Berlusconi and the time of his political good fortune. The worst would have stayed, and that was one of the many things I was wrong about.

STATEMENT OF DEFENSE

Concerning what happened in Padova the 21th September 2019 in Piazza della Frutta.

I was just passing by through the square while I was having a long walk around the city centre. It was drizzling and in the centre of the square there were women and some children. I glimpsed the Flag of Northern League party and I stopped. I didn't run towards them immediately; I didn't want to approach them or do anything that could ruin my beautiful morning.

Then, after many years spent abroad, I heard it again. I stayed still listening to it for several minutes. The same, old, devastating silence of this town. Silence.

The silence that allowed the buses of this town to be segregated for many years, my entire youth years. A segregation not legal, not forced. The segregation wanted, claimed and implemented by constant acts of aggression against women and children (very rarely men) daring, choosing to sit between white passengers.

Silence allowed it.

The silence turned immigrant workers into slaves in our restaurants, with no contract and no future, subjects of an inhuman and indecent treatment.

Silence allowed it.

Eventually, the last step of this descent into the worst: the decision of local authorities where the Northern League is in charge to take away the food in schools from immigrants' children, a decision clearly taken to discriminate against immigrant children, usually coming from disadvantaged families. There is no doubt that there can be Italian families with the very same economic issues. Nevertheless, living in their own country means those families are surrounded by a network of relatives, friends and acquaintances that prevent them from being, except in extremely difficult situations, unable to pay for school meals. Not the same, obviously, for immigrant families, out of their community, surrounded by a world that doesn't speak their language and doesn't help them to integrate at least enough to interrelate with the institutions. Wherever they ask for help they face employees and administration officers who, following a policy indulged by local Northern League politicians, make every necessity an unsolvable problem, an unanswered question. Those families don't have anyone around as their church, a relative, a friend to ask for a little help.

Furthermore, missed payments for school meals has never been claimed from Italian families, for reasons related to the constitutional right of the minor to be protected and helped by the institutions in the name of his well-being and health, as well as his right to socialise and not feel discriminated in a important moment of sharing like a meal. It was considered an attempt on the mental and physical health of the child and clearly against the letter of article 2 of the Fundamental Principle of the Italian Constitution. Not to mention the "economic and social solidarity" of article 3 that, at least for the safety of a child, should always be implemented. I would like to briefly note that the Constitution says "inviolable right of the man" and man, not citizen, following a modern wording connected to the events preceding its drafting and for which Italy was responsible during the 2nd World War.

And all over that, silence.

I went there in full possession of my faculties. I didn't insult them. I called them fascist, racist, antisemites, I didn't use any other words or definitions.

Immigrant children, in this region, are discriminated against in the schools: food is taken away from them in front of the other children. I can't imagine a clearer definition of what fascism, nazism and racism represent in this World.

I wish that an act of kindness had been granted to me: because I called them antisemites, I wish someone could have bothered Liliana Segre, Auschwitz survivor under police protection after the insults and threats received by Northern League voters and representatives. Please ask her if anti-Semitism is a word that can be used to describe an actual reality within the Northern League or if I need warning to stop speaking lies out loud.

That's what I said, with all my strength and all my voice, as it's our sacred duty to do so when the fundamental values are at stake. Anti-fascism doesn't get whispered, but cried to the sky.

Finally, a remark on the basic freedom of speech and expression. Those rights belong to everyone but when free demonstrations of freedom and critics are labelled as defamation we should ask ourselves: "who were those rights created for?" Those who get along with power, or for those who criticise it? For those who never wanted to upset the men in charge or for those breaking the rules in the name of truth or justice? For those who are afraid to be considered rude or those who are afraid to be considered complicit?

In the light of what's above, I believe it was my right to do what I did, without even considering the jurisprudence clearly speaking in favour of a more substantial defence of the individual citizen and his freedom of expression when he faced political movements and parties representing the government in charge at the time of the facts.

Then I need to address what happened with the man approaching me during my protest. There's not much to say. He violated my personal space talking to me like a poor teenager seeking attention. It was a vulgar condescendence and I spat in his face. To be clear, I reject any attempt to talk to me from above a pedestal.

I would like to end my defence with some very significant words, not mine of course. Those words are for those who think to justify their actions hiding behind laws, regulations, reducing the idea of citizenship to a tool for discrimination of fundamental rights.

The great Hannah Arendt, to explain the guilt of those who massacred many innocents following orders (so it's clear: extermination is just the last step of legal discrimination) said: "nobody has the right to obey."

INTERLUDE. LEGALITY AND RATIONAL THINKING: RAPID APPROACH

Good immigrants and bad immigrants, working immigrants and criminal immigrants: people love these distinctions.

It was curious for us, denizens of the silent undergrowth of our small city, to know the truth. As teenagers we were placed at an ideal and safe point to see what was happening around us. The main reason for that was that anything bad could happen to us: for unknown reasons police in those years had opted for a general policy of tolerance towards the use of marijuana. I still remember my boyfriend of those years picking me up at school smoking a joint in the middle of the street, a few meters from the city police department.

With us were the drug dealers, most of them boys our age, in their twenties or younger, few older than twenty-five. We were living our time in the drug business in peace, probably due to the very use of the substance. Anyway, our view from there was crystal-clear.

They didn't steal our jobs; none of us were interested in pursuing the drug dealer career and they had no chance of getting the kind of jobs most of us where destined to do. We had our time as drug consumers, but more comfortable offices than a park at night was waiting for us, somewhere.

We knew they weren't making a lot of money. They were surviving, helping their families abroad at the same time.

Their identification documents were in perfect order to avoid trouble; not exactly activists for human rights, not even politically engaged. They couldn't care less about our policy.

This river of our little lives flowed like an underground stream in the night of the parks, under the railroad bridge, through the trampled weeds on the riverbank.

You didn't see them during the day. Instead you would sit at your desk, listening to a conservative, racist teacher replying to objections you hadn't made, while looking around you realizing all your classmates are watching you. Yes, you. I mean, you are the objection. Your existence, you being there among the others. You are dramatically losing points at the social approval pageant. I keep thinking about a poem by writer Cesare Pavese which I can't forget; the sash of Miss Anomaly just bothers me swinging from the chair. I scribble on my agenda and ask myself why I am sober. When I will learn? Jesus, When?

TRIBUTE TO ANTIPATHY (OR ABOUT THE TRAGIC MISTAKE OF BEING GOOD)

Facing the violence and brutality of racism, it is understandable to feel a duty to say the right thing.

That can be difficult, if you're alone.

It's much easier when someone is watching. When we post something on our social media or we can think about people speaking in a TV talk show. Such goodness! Such a big heart! A marvellous candy pink ocean of noble sentiments and inner beauty.

But the glittery surface waves of this giant jar of honey hide a world of dark, deep, unspeakable lies. I've always asked myself why we tell ourselves those lies. Primarily, why we let others tell us lies. The explanation came, simple and terrible, on a rainy day like many others here in England. I was home alone in front of my little mirror in my tiny house. I was enjoying the quiet of a clean moment all for myself, staying home and dedicating some time to little useless things I love to alleviate the weight of a week of work. I was thinking that I deserved some rest. It was a long time since I 'd taken a moment for myself. I couldn't recall for how long I had lived that life. I came back from work, like many others, after hours of hard work; and like many others I barely had the physical strength to make my dinner and prepare for the following day. I struggled to read a book, a newspaper. I was always tired. I took care of my body, my bones, those hands that work and earn money. I needed to live in different dimensions other than work and money and bills and tiresomeness. My heart was asking more but I couldn't give any more. Almost trying to score points, I was about to write something on Twitter about Italian racism. I just stopped for a second. It was so comforting for me being able to do at least this little thing. But.. how much good was I doing to the anti-racism cause? Not much. Nothing, probably.

So it occurred to me that the most relevant dimension of life I needed to get back was out there, in the streets, between people where the confrontation can be harder than an online soliloquy, but where the change I want to speak of must happen. I see this idea is not shared by many at the moment. I can clearly see the moral more than the physical convenience of a virtual social life. This vortex of laziness and apathy has already become what becomes of everything this world creates: a market trend. The commercialization of indignation is the current stage in which the public opinion thinks it can survive and still be meaningful. But with commercialization ideas die and business grows. It's a pathetic world where public figures of all kind jump from compassionate messages of peace to fashion show in a continuum that leaves us pleasantly confused and comforted by words of hope and a lot of glitter. The world out there is not going to change. It's missing what has always been necessary for the course of history to change: sacrifice.

Our governments, hungry for power and money, know this very well. None of them ever objected to an event whose revenues would be devolved to feed children of a poor country. Politicians only listened to the requests of people just when it became clear that the population was ready to sacrifice days of salary, reputation, business to protest until they obtain what they asked for; when everything in a country stops off because nothing makes sense anymore without that right to protest.

Politics, of course, was different too. This is the age of antidemocratic authoritarianism, the night of the umpteenth genocide. In India, at the moment. Myanmar, too. With a Nobel Peace Price to give her blessing to torturers.

It's also our fault. It's the most devastating product capitalists are able to sell us : the after-dinner political engagement: the illusion that we are politically relevant in a world that is not the real one. Because in the real world of money and business, capitalism rules without question. We are only allowed in the harmless virtual space. But there, in the mix of common problems and individual stories, the discourse easily skips from political debate to individual criticism. Often destructive, vicious; a criticism as furious online as we're powerless in real political life.

Or the opposite: absolute reverence, the blind devotion we need to fill up with virtual noble intentions and forget how inept and indifferent and ignorant we are in the streets of our cities. How absent are our efforts to stop and care about what happens to real immigrants: women, children who live near us, out of the moving Instagram pictures?

Our life should change at least a bit. We could stop our walk to our last purchase and appreciate the value of taking a stand not just for us, but for the many lives affected by our indifference. Try thinking about that child who's watching its mother being insulted and mistreated as if he were our own son. Doing for him what we wish would be done for *our* children. Instead, it's so easy to say that I am so radical and am exaggerating things. But you're good, you're still good because you clap at every compassionate show they serve you. Shiny and composed shows, sold and digested in the greedy belly of our egos, the cradle of our hypocrisy.

This hideous layer of intentional blindness hides a quite simple truth that leaves us with no pleasant alternatives: the dialogue between different political views isn't always possible. A common base is necessary or the dialogue we seek in the name of democracy becomes a pale farce, just good to gain votes and consent and, above all, economic power.

To have a real dialogue two conditions are needed: a willingness to have a rational debate and a common objective.

Concerning the will for an actual dialogue, I would like someone to look at the last 25 years of Italian politics with the Northern League in charge with Ministers in several governments and tell me if the smallest indication of a willingness to have a serious discussion can be seen. For instance, we can try to evaluate how the League deals with the statements and attitudes of its members and elected representatives. In the Veneto region the League won the election with 60%. It's a region where the League has a long history in the local administration of the region and several of its cities. Does someone really think bringing this region to the edge of savagery where men attack women and children is a sign of dialogue from them? Mediation? Moderation? I deeply doubt it.

The second condition is the common values we should aim to reach through dialogue. If we head in different directions, we can talk to each other to feel better but it doesn't make any sense. The objective of any political movement in a democratic state is the attainment of the ideals of economic well-being and justice that, in Italy, are sanctioned by our Constitution. Can someone say the Northern League has as its main political aim the values of equality and justice our Constitution grants to us? No one is going to risk ridicule by asserting this.

It doesn't matter. This evil is here, and we must be ready to speak out and fight. Our voice must be heard by those who plot to bring racism to our streets with no consequences. But many people seem to ignore how and why to rebel. We must ask ourselves how this happened.

I think it has been a tragic mistake to think that the right-minded and their eternal willingness for dialogue no-matter-what were so comforting and that, even if we know nothing is going to change at the end of the day, they meant no harm. There has never been anything wrong with being good persons. I couldn't disagree more.

The one thing necessary for our soul to survive and this night to end is a healthy dose of antipathy. This is not only about social media. In Veneto the others acceptance is considered proportional to how right you are and being a voice out of the chorus is just a symptom of your problems, your egocentrism. The reassuring common opinion wants to gently wrap you and doesn't like being rejected. And it's when you do so, moving away from them, that you need antipathy; that healthy malevolence keeping you alert, waiting for them to try again with you, weird thing. You: different and so, obviously, wrong. The creepy Nazi snakes in our daily lives. Don't bother to ask, they don't care! Why do you think we care so much? We don't! Which to be honest doesn't explain why they are so aggressive, verbally violent, intolerant... quite an effort, for people who don't care.

We kept believing a dialogue was possible while they were taking the problematic mental health of the worse pathetic loser drunk of our neighbourhood and turning it into a political program. Considering them to be a legitimate part of the public debate as a subtle attempt to help them toward, I would say, civilization, didn't work. But in response to this reality, we didn't choose to confront them. We hid in the pink cloud of charities and sustainability conferences, because it's so optimistic to think we still can do something, even if it's just to clap at another, adorable, beneficient event. The saddest thing is that those who are feeding us these lies are the same Left we have been looking to for answers. Left-wing politics was supposed to be the politics of the Other, the Different. Today the left parties are languishing in the hands of power-seeking grey figures whose only strategy is to imitate the right and move another step further to the right at every election , hoping to gain consent and so, power. Leftist politicians and their good intentions and beautiful words on social media freed themselves from the obligation of actually doing something and leave us in a world of virtual victories.

When everything counts but the result of your actions, all is just a big circus: a merry-go-round of accusations, replicas, futile hopes and useless scandals: good sentiments without the rough skin of conviction. A continuous run for consent that rewards the best sellers of smoke and *pret a porter.*

ANOTHER SOLDIER

No one knew when and why he would start. Although everyone loved him, it was not easy for any of listening to the same story dozens of times. Except for me. I should have realized at that time I had my problems: I liked to hear his story endless times.

That's why I didn't mind and sometimes I wondered around my grandfather, my mother's father, hoping that, seeing someone to chat with, he might think of telling me a little more about the war.

It was exciting, as if he had lived something so terribly real, at the time when things were not being told in books or by those who remembered them, but they actually happened. For as long as I can remember I've had this feeling of living on the margins of someone else's life. Elders, who remembered when the town was vibrant and not a place from which people were just leaving; my young aunts, who were starting to live their whole lives in a beautiful new home; or my parents, who had experienced the time when politicians weren't all old and hadn't already done their worst.

I was a lovely child, but I struggled if someone paid attention to me. Feeling invisible made me independent and joyful. I didn't pay attention to anything that didn't draw my interest, and I loved to hear stories. Grandfather's stories were not bad at all. Moreover, for me, semi-autistic of repetition, hearing those stories once a year was not even an actual reoccurrence.

The last time I remember listening to his story was in my grandparents bedroom. Grandfather had asked me to make their bed with him and I was helping him where his sight couldn't reach. You had to remain nearby in silence for a while, leave his mind running silently toward the only memories left after three strokes which had hit him badly; the cardiologist told us he had the heart of a bull.

So he would start, smiling, looking at a black point as he slowly began to stutter few words. Then you had to look at him in silence, without haste or whatever could have made him uncomfortable; an old man speaking to himself, giving only annoyance...

Then the stuttering became a word, his smile got malicious while his eyes wandered over the sand of North Africa, staring at that blond young man and his blue eyes; small but pretty young man, as he used to call the men of his own race, running among the other soldiers in the opposite direction to where the enemies were coming from.

As long as there were only the British on the enemy front, Italian soldiers of the fascist regime were sometimes advancing, sometimes withdrawing. They went on like this for a while, so the situation was rather uncertain and boring. One day they suddenly heard a noise coming up into the sky and everyone was staring up, trying to understand what was going on. Then so many planes appeared, flying over their heads in such numbers that they made shadow in the sky. The Americans had joined the war, and since then there had been no further advancing and withdrawal. They were done with boredom.

They turned in the opposite direction to the front line and did nothing but run for days. This was literally the war my grandfather remembered, but it wasn't the war he had fought.

In his real life, back in the past, he was in one of the Italian Army divisions that fought in the well-known battle of Tobruk.

The battle was against the Australian and the British

army in Libya. When Tobruk was left to the Allies, the division moved from Libya to Egypt where they fought and lost in El Alamein.

The Battle of El Alamein decided the fate of the North African front, where the Allied troops were not always in a large majority but certainly had better equipment. When the Italian and German troops surrendered, about 20,000 Italian soldiers doubled back to the coast in an attempt to escape, but they were taken prisoner and deported to North America. There, my grandfather was imprisoned in various different detention camps around the U.S. for about 4 years.

This detention in the United States was one of the most serene times of his life; America seemed to him a lively country engaged in an economic progress that would have made the USA the "America the immigrants dream of."

He lived somewhere in California for a while, just admiring the sun-blessed skyscrapers under construction: the sun only promised prosperity, after the atrocities of the war.

Then he was transferred to a place whose name he remembered as Florence. It turns out there was a town named Florence in Arizona with a WW II prisoners' camp nearby.

He told us it was one of the best time of his life, but he decided to come back, although he had always had clean clothes and worked in the best conditions possible given the situation, despite the constant supply of unnecessary goods such as sweets and cigarettes (I assume that alcohol was also used, but grandad was never a drinker), and even though everyone treated him with respect, and the rooms where they slept or eat were more than acceptable. I never understood why he never regretted coming back, even when the moment arrived and he just found a whole country destroyed and his small village in ruins.

He used to shake his head and say it was pitiful to see black people: always working in the camps, dirty, malnourished, abused all the time. It was a vision he couldn't stand.

He wasn't a civil rights activist but rather a very simple man, but he didn't understand racism. Before outrage, he couldn't explain it. He was a man from the deep south, as they say, but he understood that human violence could not be underestimated, and that society was expressing violence.

That fascist soldier would have lived with difficulty surrounded by the violence of one side and the suffering of the other. He was a peaceful human being, not one who could survive where people beat, exploit and discriminate relentlessly against other people. He came back and did what he was meant to do, never wishing for himself anything else. He married the nicest girl in the town and had four children.

When I was a teenager, I watched him telling this story for the umpteenth time. I felt I was born from there. I had that gene, the allergy to other people's suffering. I was proud to come from there. I never thought of him as a fascist soldier.

He talked about the deportation of Jewish people just saying "poor people, we shouldn't have done it". No, we shouldn't.

He was a simple man. After fascism and the experience of hate and war, he voted Communist for the rest of his life.

Grandma nodded. She agreed communists were the "only ones there to defend us", the poor ones. She agreed while carefully organizing her trip on Sunday to Naples, because the bishop was taking confession and "I had to go, because I got four children, all of them Communists". She voted Communist herself; it could be forgiven by God from a religious woman like her. But their sons, they needed a good word from her.

Then in the 1990s, we began to hear about the mafia, politics, the masonry and the American secret services activities in Italy . Grandad shook his head one day, wiping his mouth with a napkin during a summer lunch: "we're poor people, we don't understand these things".

CRY, BABY CRY .

"War is, primarily and everywhere, an institutional disaster, the sinking of the juridicial system, that condition in which people pursue their rights through violence. All those who experienced the world, specially the modern world, know that the breaking in of violence means in the first place the eradication of every rule of behavior and juridicial system...". Those are the words of Fredric Maurice, International Red Cross delegate killed in Sarajevo the 19th May, 1992. They describe the whole world in which the 13 year- old little girl walked.

Her house is not hers anymore, her parents have been killed. In that little corner of the world her skinny legs walk through destruction, absorbing at every step the awareness that in war there's no help or salvation. No number to call, no police or social workers. The monopolisation of violence by legal authorities is sand in the wind. No one is going to look for you.

She sought shelter and found it. I know it, because I know she lost it, later. Then she couldn't walk anymore. She was caught and imprisoned in a concentration camp. There might have been an echo in her mind. "Who I am now and why this is happening to me? What will I be able to be if I wake up after falling asleep again?" The desperation of a child, absolute as the inner icy silence, because your mind can't understand the meaning of power through someone else's torture. The greed for power of those little men who lived their poor lives, for years, in the semi obscurity of their certitude.

Long before the war was, the first time you felt it crawling under your skin: every night, and night after night. Being a no-one because you can't be otherwise. You were born useless and raised worse. But you are the only one to deeply understand your mediocrity, in the shadow of the others' honesty, bravery and beauty. In the brief instant of your conception a crumb of mental disability flew like a feather into the soul of a good man instead of yours. To know what you are and being unable to understand much more than this, that's your problem. Yours, ours. Distorted from indecency, you chopped the fragile thread crime by crime. Now, in time of war, you're free: from principles, dignity, decency. Horror is grand, I am the horror.

Raping is primarily having the power to do it. Power. It's what happened to this little girl, for weeks victim of the deepest misery. Avoidable, unforgivable, eternal.

She has been released in a prisoners exchange. International Red Cross certifies in a brief note. I held the paper between my fingers as though I didn't want to cause it harm. I read once again and the words seem written by a horrified bureaocraut. Someone who must write about a life torn apart and hurries to forget and move on.

Today I look at her: the child is grown up. She is tall and has a child in her arms. Sitting down next to me, she just cuddled her son, gave him a kiss while having a look at the other two. There's nothing spontaneous in those actions. I just realized she doesn't look natural because she doesn't smile when people usually do . She doesn't speak either: her husband talks for her. I don't really listen what he's saying cause I know their problem already and what the woman here with me is trying to do for them. I just breath slowly, waiting for the minutes to pass and take me out of here, far from this egg of silence in which she lives. She shakes my hand looking in my eyes when she introduces herself. She looks straight into my eyes but doesn't see me. My reflection doesn't arrive at her dark eyes in the form of an emotional reaction to a new person whatsoever. I am not even here. I can vaguely see tears floating in her eyes. Maybe. She is speechless, lost in the horrors of the past, but also in the present life that should have been salvation and instead it's just a *plan de vol,* the decision of Swiss authorities to send her back to Sarajevo and to the high chance of being assassinated by her torturers still on the loose. Her house today is an empty room with some chairs, no table and 3 beautiful children. I look at her and I can tell there is no coming back from her blind desperation. She doesn't see, she doesn't cry or smile neither. She's not here. She's there, in a cell behind the barbed wire, alone and violated.

I kept my lips pursed so they wouldn't shake. A date makes me wince. I just cough while her husband and the woman talk of how to manage the period of secrecy waiting for journalist and a politician in Geneva to take an interest in the case. I regain control, I don't move. My same year of birth. We're the same age.

I lived my share of this life. I had my years of cold and hunger, but I've never been afraid. A world without war fed me and my family on hope. In our empty house, even without the essentials we needed, we were hopeful and happy.

She gives the little ones to the father. She takes the hands of the other two with kindness. She doesn't want anything of me. I didn't try to talk to her. There is no common language to fill this distance. I have no anchor as salvation for her drift.

I turn my attention to the two still speaking. The situation they're facing reminds me of a documentary on the sounds of the Shoah and Moni Ovadia talking about the music the Auschwitz prisoners were forced to play and listen to: silly little tunes, derisive of their suffering. And him saying : "We should never forget the Nazi dimension of travesty. Monstrous, but still travesty." Christoph Blocher, xenophobe Swiss politician and head of the Ministry of Justice, explained his decision by asking for what reason the child, once out of the concentration camp, didn't fly immediately abroad? For him, the fact that she stayed in Bosnia is evidence that she didn't and doesn't risk anything in her country. For this reason she can be repatriated.

In that privileged corner of the World, under the cold, bored Sun of the peaceful north European spring, I find myself without warning in front of a victim of a war crime.

I didn't say anything, I focused on not shaking and controlling what my hands where doing.

"Direction" has always been an important meaning for me. Where my words and my decisions go, even the smallest ones. But since that encounter, my stubborness became an untiring peace of mind, even pleasant.

Liliana Segre remembers still today the emotional tribute the inmates of Milano's prison reserved for her and the other innocent Jewish citizens, when they slowly started to walk out of the prison to be sent to Auschwitz. A scarf, a glove, a piece of bread or a biscuit, flying through the cell bars onto their heads. And the voices of the guilty ones, last and rejected, blow out in the open the only words of truth spoken those days in the silent, coward Milano: "you're innocents! You don't deserve this! You didn't do anything! Don't give up! God bless you!" It was the blessing of the guilty, guilty and still men, speaking the truth.

It's so difficult to expect something from ourselves when it comes to fight. But this story made me realize how much we can do, and be, without aspiring to perfection. If I could be just a guilty hand behind bars throwing a scarf to the innocents sent to die!

I was anything like that when I met her. Walking out of the cafeteria I felt just calm. Relieved and quiet. There is something deeply right in this fight, and I live through those difficult times with no fear since then. I don't want to win arguments or show off intellectual flawlessness. I wake up and ask myself if I am ready to say and to do, to stay and to fight. Be the annoying one. Be bad.

I wish not to see her dark, dried eyes for the rest of my life, though. But please cry, baby, cry.

Thank you to my dear friend Mattia, for all the support and for being much more unusual than me.

Thanks to all the Spiffing Covers team, for the professionality they were able to put in this little project even in those very difficult times. I am glad I found you, guys.

www.ingramcontent.com/pod-product-compliance
Lightning Source LLC
Chambersburg PA
CBHW071804140825
31095CB00045B/831